Late Gifts

RICHARD PRICE

T0059490

CARCANET POETRY

First published in Great Britain in 2023 by
Carcanet
Alliance House, 30 Cross Street
Manchester, M 2   7 AQ
www.carcanet.co.uk

A CIP catalogue record for this book is
available from the British Library.

ISBN 978 1 80017 349 1

Book design by Andrew Latimer, Carcanet
Typesetting by LiteBook Prepress Services
Printed in Great Britain by SRP Ltd, Exeter, Devon

The publisher acknowledges financial
assistance from Arts Council England.

LATE GIFTS

Richard Price is Head of Contemporary British Collections at the British Library and a tutor at the Poetry School, London. He has published over a dozen books of poetry since his debut in 1993, including *Lucky Day* (2005), which was a *Guardian* Book of the Year and shortlisted for the Whitbread Poetry Prize. In 2012 his poem 'Hedge Sparrows' was chosen to represent Team GB in the Olympics project 'The Written World'. A year later, *Small World* (2012) won the Creative Scotland Award in his home country. It was followed by another *Guardian* Book of the Year, *Moon for Sale* (2017), which was also shortlisted for the Saltire Society Poetry Book of the Year. Price's re-telling of Inuit stories in *The Owner of the Sea* (2021) was a *Scotsman* Book of the Year.

CONTENTS

WHAT THEY FOUND ON THE BEACH

SHORE GIFTS

LOSING THE WORD 'LOVE'

SHORE THEFTS

AFTER WORDS

LAST WORD

Some of these poems have been published in *And Other Poems, Bad Lilies,* Nancy Campbell's *A Book of Banished Words, The Caught Habits of Language: an Entertainment for W.S. Graham* (edited by Rachael Boast, Andy Ching and Nathan Hamilton), *The Dark Horse, Finished Creatures, Magma, Mayday, PN Review, Poetry Review, The Rialto, Spark: Poetry and Art Inspired by the Novels of Muriel Spark* (edited by Rob A. Mackenzie and Louise Peterkin), *The Times Literary Supplement,* and *Verseville.* My thanks to the editors and other publishing workers involved and to dear, patient, friends who have read and commented upon versions of this book.

My particular thanks to the Society of Authors for an Authors' Foundation Award which helped pay towards childcare at a critical time.

In loving memory of Tim Price, 1961–2021

For Rory

We are the artists of the dream.
We are the Baddies.
We twist ears into eyebrows.

Rory Price-Lowe

LATE GIFTS

NOBODY'S CHILD

her child
who is my child
as holy
as loved
as inner thought

my child
who is her child
no-one's child
hush   thought is
waking

our child   no-one's child
who has been dreaming
(now woken)   forgetting
a future world   remembering
a new world   nobody's child

SOMEBODY'S CHILD

CHILDREN ARE WILD

Children are wild and make dens with coats and a folding table
in one-room bed-and-breakfasts.

There are kids' homes in the condemned woods.
Black polythene flaps like a wood-gatherer in a glimpse of distance.
One lean-to has the wet weight of silver birches for structural timber.
There's stolen ply, too, orange as 'just a little milk in tea, thanks', and neat handwriting.
An ex-soldier has settled in the shelter of a tree-house with its car-door shut. All autumn
he lays high but now everything's gone bar the cut leaf of a SIM, two turquoise sandals, and an empty
holdall.

The automatic doors are half opening, half closing.
Just outside on the cheer-us-up paving there's a, a
middle-aged man sitting air-drumming, a quick light
percussion, onset of Parkinson's perhaps.
He's folded back the four black/blue petals
of an empty Happy Meal box to…
make a begging cup – kicked now, crushed
by the white puffy trainers
of a man shouting You
shall not enter! You
shall not enter
the Kingdom
of God!
Die!

Die!
and God
tells Sportsman
to Set the fake
on fire, so he clicks,
clicks his purple lighter,
clicks, clicks close, but no flame, God
is testing the man, Urinate
on the fake, God says quite politely
so Sportsman is flipping his penis out.
Now a woman from above Explore Learning
shouts down Put it away! You cunt! I'm calling the,
you fucking low life, get away from him, I'm dialling –
she holds up the pink phone. He flees like he's being hunted.

SOMEBODY'S CHILD

Thrown
wide out –
in the bins
a Pole working
at Costa daytime
spends nights cooking up, then,
neat alarm clock set, beds down
between Landfill and Recycling.
Six months in he's gaunt but smiles Welcome.
Above him low-seat drivers ramp fast up
to easyGym for 24hr protein
shakes, spinning classes, lycra retro dance, dumbells
v donuts. (In the flats five floors high the air is fuel –
children inhale snags of petrol, diesel, plane fumes, flicked dust.)

CITY ALLOTMENT

Hasan sub-leases a second plot
and to hell with the red tape.

Phil swears in Italian.
He shares seedling and fruit.

Dennis grows irises
and some men call him Flower Boy.

Elaine is as neat as a diagram.
She colours-in borders with lavender.

Joy and Honor
keep themselves to themselves.

Hasan was Hussein, but Iraq.
Covid took him.

It's Spring and his widow says
one plot is enough.

LEFT-HAND DRIVE

Stolen left-hand drive, bench front-seat.
Europe or America? Kraftwerk? Harmonica? Contrast / compete.
Choose the ready-made real
as you wake up at the wheel, a child in Cuban heels, The Fall on repeat.

It's wayback when or maybe the day after next week.
Rituals and coins, jump-cuts and joins, now you hear her speak.
But you miss the big reveal
when you wake up at the wheel: half robot, half antique.

The fires have cleared and you're miles from lake and peak.
Moonscape, ocean floor? Airstrip? Charcoal moor? You're way too weak
to know if you can heal
but you wake up at the wheel, wrong kind of unique.

Your dreams are at the tip of your tongue.
You know there's oil – in the aqualung.
You spy the mime but what gets sung?
What's the pretty-little-deal?
                    as you wake up at the wheel.

"The slave trade," she says, "makes suave transactions.
The police and politicians, the press and all the rest,
are proud to be the faction
of greed: they watch the blood congeal.
They connive, collect, conceal,"
                    and you wake up at the wheel.

You don't know the voice but you love the mouth and speech,
their playlist, their pliers, the way they seem to teach
the invention of steel,
and how to wake up at the wheel – at the final beach.

An ecstatic insect, a twitching leaf.
Which one's you she says, half-grin, half-grief,
but you refuse the windscreen ideal.
When you wake up at the wheel you cry in disbelief.

You keep your own counsel so it makes you hard to reach.
You're way too fast but she doesn't want to preach
or joke or kneel
so you wake up at the wheel when the tyres start to screech.

You have dreams. The bell can't be rung.
If this is home it's false, too close, too far-flung.
You bide your time until you're stung
by an emblematic bee, by reluctant, indignant, zeal,
                    and you wake up at the wheel.

You have to stop the stares and the schoolroom slaughter.
Now you're underground, or it could be underwater.
You're the star of the children's ordeal,
a god with mass appeal,
no, wait, a crab in a tightening creel
                    as you wake up at the wheel.

The road is too rivery for same day delivery and the crate has lost its seal.
It spills space-rocks and a platinum ring, gaskets and masochist string,
brisket of lab-grown lamb, *Lurex*, latex, and the *I Ching*,
a yoga mat and a cuddly eel.

It spills smallpox in phials and a syringe,
anthrax pamphlets from yesterday's fringe,
dog baskets, dope and body-positive bling,
slops of butter from Kerry, rip-offs of Chuck Berry, his My Ding-a-ling,
a cricket bat, a baseball cap and a bubbling Happy Meal.

It spills sparkle socks and a paling Tam Lin, limpets and cleats,
trumpets and receipts, laminated reviews of the Rite of Spring.
It spills kompromat and Complan, a tiny Jane and Tarzan,
sawn-off-tusks, custard dust, civet musk in a Silk Road sling,
and jars of talismatic apple-peel.

(A mechanical box slips and drops: it spills the ticks and tocks
of unscented seconds and ting.
There are uncensored voices and recorded rejoices
                              for the Once and Future King,
a llama hat, lamprey, and leggings (too thin)
and there are eggs exuded from crocodile and teal.)

It spills freesias, anti-amnesias, gifts for forgiveness, a children's swing.
There are hard-earned earrings, video'd hearings
        (a witness minded his own business then opted to sing).
It spills self-help, help-your-self'd from the shelves of a selfless bookmobile.
It spills palm oil for mouthfeel.

It spills blueboy phlox and stuffed vine-leaves in a tin.
It spills tea and electronics, heavy avionics, voodoo for Brent from Beijing,
and a thermostat and veal.

It spills savoury chocs and sculptures from old Benin.
It spills sacred caskets discovered in spa-lets (one had been a night-club bin)
and notes of how people voted and a sim card loaded
                              with a twice-encoded squeal.

It spills old locks and a new kind of spring,
                              anklets with love-heart and golden wing,
a lucky cat with paw in pained appeal.
It spills a throat-slit fox in mid-grin, muskets for Mohawks, advice
    for the Inca
                              (how Christians must sing),
a technocrat's guestimate, a diplomat's testament and the last harbour seal.

It's starting to be surreal.
The sky comes over all shivery above the hearse's livery –
you're just realising you're both the man driving
and the corpse twitching within.
You're the ancient wiseacre – No, a toddler with a pacemaker,
and "Baby's just grazed his shin".

A man plays lollipops on a glockenspiel.
You sniff, you cough – you might have nodded off. You try to be genteel –
and you wake up at the wheel.

She wouldn't cross a picket line and neither would I.
We agreed on politics but couldn't see eye to eye
on how to feel.
We said Goodbye to keep the closeness real
and I woke up at the wheel.

LAST DAY OF THE LEAGUE
in memory, Murdo Price, 1989-2016

Something wrong, tone, a hesitation, his voice quieter,
"Last day of the League, it's always a Sunday."
All my life my brother's been teaching me football.
Now he says But yeah come over, bring the boy.
At the entry-phone I speak and no word
just doorframe buzz and we're up the stairs,
find his door open and he's home,
tv on, all fine, and I goes
What's the game and he
tells me, and he says
Last day of the League,
Murdo loved
this, that
boy.

LATE GIFTS

LATE GIFT

That wooden gift
needed
to be a 'real boy' –

halfway between 'it'
and 'who', done-to
and does, a toy

between timber and finger,
loved and loves.

            But the need in his maker,
            the old carpenter, was stronger –

            it was the need,
            this need, this need,
            to be a real father.

LANDLADY WHO WORKS FOR THE BBC

a shadow at the door edge
      is a shape at the door edge
            is a quantity rapid across the carpet

is a rat beneath the cot

Baby's up with us we are not believing
      we are believing
            are phoning   Landlady-who-works-for-the-BBC

who is not believing
      who is believing but it's a mouse surely
            everyone has them   you're young you don't know these things

ok it is a rat let's not get hysterical   it will be acting alone

      have you been keeping my property clean
            you've been eating crisps haven't you

much later we'll find the bone of a cuttlefish
is unique   an inside shell (keeps it buoyant)

we'll praise the three hearts and jet propulsion
we'll play as if we were that   creature
(superheroes with turquoise blood)

superheroes full of explosions, incendiary ink
sticky old photographs, liquid fog
I'm blind! I'm blind!

but right now my arm aches   could it be replaced with wood
carbon-fibre in the upgrade   when when when will baby sleep
clean out of

       so what eases him just wide of wide-awake
       is the hairdryer   the temperate creature at the bedside
       turned away   (Love Will Tear Us Apart)
       life-saver   Lullaby Electrique

now I'm clicking the machine off
still holding the human package
rocking him, keeping up the fro-and-to

is he is he is he

and I think of the crouching shape
a hairdryer   a cuttlefish   and he does let go of the day
and I promise myself   (it'll be years later)
when he's five say   we'll look it up together   cuttlefish
you know, when he asks   how do hairdryers work, Dad

HAVE YOU GOT A NOSE?

Have you got a nose?
Have you got a nose?
Yes, you've got one of those.   [touch own nose]

Have you got an ear?
Have you got an ear?
Yes, I can see one here.   [touch own ear]

Have you got some eyes?
Have you got some eyes?
Yes, a ni-i-ice surprise.   [reveal eyes behind a hand / look left, look right]

People hurrying, January to December.
People hurrying, they forget to remember.

Have you got some toes?
Have you got some toes?
Yes, I-'ve g-o-t some of those.   [point to toes]

ORANGUTAN

Orang-u-tan! Orang-u-tan!

Swaying in the trees.
Bouncing in the breeze.
Flicking all the fleas.
Licking all the toe cheese!

Orang-u-tan! Orang-u-tan!

THE CUB

He is a poor sleeper.
He is disturbed by his own red coat. It waits at the end of the radiator.
In this light he can't see it's red but he's absorbed the fact of its colour.
He is afraid of Little Red Riding Hood, not the wolf.
He wants the safety of the forest
which he senses in the perfume of the timber of his parents' double bed.
The scent twists back to ancient woodland across the islands,
across the waking continent,
                                        further,
to Gilgamesh when he was ruthless and to the aromatic kingdom of
    Humbaba
where the ratio of respect to persecution favoured the wolves.

Even half asleep he is polite,
a little boy opening his bedroom door carefully
                                        and then pausing,
                                                closing it carefully after himself,
and then, and only then, rushing into his parents' room, launching himself
at us, cosying himself in.
He directs his father's hand to his midriff which is cold.
(I think: we must order him new pyjamas in the morning, and also:
will I remember this thought in the morning?)

All move, adjusting to life in the den.
All allow themselves a return – to the reality of their dreams,
to their natural impersonation of a hunting pack asleep.

NEW ELECTRIC PIANO

I don't know
why I don't
call out
but I
open the door
quietly.
I softly
know the
rooms again.

The lives are sleeping.

(I check my phone
to check my phone:
is there any news
about the news?)

In the front room
a boy my son
naps across
the armchair.
He's so tall
he's had to
fold himself in.

In our bedroom
a woman you
nearly a stranger
has finally left
a bright shore.
The blinds have
been darkened
to full sail.

She, don't say she,
faces away
and I'm greedy
to wake you, to
kiss as if my kiss
could be more
important
than rest, the
privacy of sleep.

(I check my phone
to check my phone:
is there any news
about the news?)

I leave you,
I walk
into my son's
empty room.
It's chocka
with ons and
offs, with
greens and whites,
the slick reds
of shaped plastic,
with mimics,
with machines.

I'm outsize on the interstellar bed.

(I check my phone
to check my phone:
any news
about the news?)

Later the
almost stranger
who is you
tells me
the peace

is all about the piano:
the boy
just fell asleep,
serene, listening
to his mother
a young woman
relearning Bach,
and she, you, you

knew then
there was time
after all
to escape.

TIDY UP THE SCENE

Frank is telling me – "The feds are on the move,
It's a black kid so they've no time to lose.
They shoot the man in his car.
Another wet-wiped local star.
The cops get their stories straight –
it's not too late
to practice what they're meant to mean
and tidy up the scene."

Frank is telling me – "The judges could not lose.
It's politics so they call it stealing shoes.
Attacking shopping's a protest too far.
The trainer's sacred, so's the bra.
Retail's endangered, unique.
Justice slurs when it starts to speak:
jail the poor to keep the righteous clean,
and tidy up the scene."

Frank is telling me – "Half the country's on my tail,
the TV and the holy *Mail* –
just for the colour of my 'tan'.
England doesn't need the Klan:
when your skin can't be trusted
your future's done-and-dusted.
It's 'empathy' and arm-lock, phone the Condolences Team,
and tidy up the scene."

Frank says softly – "Don't listen to what I'm saying –
look at the boys here playing,
thinking up a new world with laughs and Lego,
colour and creation from the chaos at the get-go.
They both start in the same circumstances –
you know the difference in their likely life chances."
    Then he calls to my boy and his Dean,
    gentle, like he's lost all spleen,
    subtle, like there's more he wants to mean
    (he makes me think I'm down there with the toys).
"Clear up now, boys! –
      No order, no ice cream!"
and "Tidy up the scene."

THE AIR THAT HE BREATHES

I have a little boy,
late gift in last days.
He laughs so freely, and that's how he plays.
He doesn't see nothing's free –
least, not the air that he breathes.

I walk with him.
I take his sticky hand.
We risk the road,
he skips to a scrap of land.
Beneath old trees refugees twitch in their sleep.
We're all 'sharing the peace' – and the air that he breathes.

There's a five-a-side field,
it's all marked down for shops and flats –
'affordable' homes, and zero rate of tax
for land-bank owner-absentees.
It's a Government decree.
There's a short-term lease on the air that he breathes.

I never thought I'd leave this world
with the children fighting for air.
I never thought I'd see this greed
and leave them choking there –
outside, at the 'gated community' wall.
I didn't think at all –
I believe the things we need should be free,
including the air that he breathes.

I have a little boy,
late gift in last days.
He laughs so freely, and that's how he plays.

Are you three ears and a nose?
Are you two lampposts mid-argument?
Are you an eyebrow and a training shoe?
Are you a robot with a cold?
Are you a yes and three no's?
Are you a whippet?
Are you a spider in a dressing gown?
Are you made of chocolate and dust?
Are you a baboon?
Are you not responsible for your own actions?
Are you a tree frog?
Are you a finger alphabet?
Are you made from the oceans?
Are you Helen Sharman?
Are you a puzzle with two pieces repeated and one piece missing?
Are you batteries included?
Are you a no and three yes's?
Are you a puppy bred as a hot water bottle for an Emperor, later deposed?
   (the Emperor)
Are you vegetarian bacon?
Are you gold and a leaf?
Are you half a hiccup?
Are you a pizza?
Are you the mention of pyjamas?
Are you a forgotten language?
Are you Master Miracle of Marmalade Mews?
Are you a plausible equation?
Are you toothpaste's ghost?
Are you scooterlific?
Are you one word for a two word concept?
Are you an egg but not a cup?

Are you the hairbrush for a mammoth?
Are you a yoghurt fish?
Are you this but not that?
Are you that but not this?
Are you just not into Snap?
Are you a trembleberry?
Are you not the half of it?
Are you a pigeon whisker?
Are you the latest dance craze?
Are you not sorry and never will be so we better just accept it?

THE ABSENCE

I tell close friends at an evening out
and there's affectionate teasing,
growing your own football team?
and I know it's early days and have I jinxed it
but joy is joy uncontained
and then the next time I say nothing,
it's not for a group conversation,
they must know from me not talking,
and I remember the news

of no heartbeat and the necessity
of the end, and holding each other,
and the week or so of blood
and the quick sorrow, we hoped,
but it wasn't quick, isn't, and my job
is to be supportive, this is
physical trauma
smack right on top of mental trauma
trauma I am here, I am supportive, am I

because this shock this grief
is asymmetrical, right,
'be the strong silent type',
this grief can't be real grief,
full grief, even I'm thinking that,
get over yourself,
my role is [   ]
and I am: look,
how strong, how silent.

x

Geology of clutter, compression. Upside-down buggy, slant, the speed of the past in small scuffed wheels. Muscle-memory flinch of metal-clip. Stiff bib, fungal bloom. Egg-blue potty / football nest. "In case we have another." Hand-me-down tees from a family friend: super-heroes in flex; huge-wheeled cars. (Our boy's tops beyond gift in a month). Child's car-seat / curved husk that won't settle. Bags, boxes, trays. Brazil rucksack. From prehistoric times: Portuguese cassettes. Breast-pump as if medical; self-help; candle cages. Spirit level on the fuse array. Patient Henry, baby elephant.

ROCK, PAPER, SCISSORS

it's the fifth day of jeopardy –
sleeping is waking & waking
is a hollowed-out dream
my ribs and my lungs
fossilise their embrace

           it's the sixth day is it
           and the news is scraps
           over toilet paper

           the pilot of an air ambulance
           is dead and young

and now the seventh
finally cuts through –

on the pavement below
there's my son and his mother   kindness

he's miming a game
rock   paper   scissors

when we match we both shout: Telepathic!

The constellations have been supporting us during the emergency. It is good to have the lad here after I've been unwell. A few nights ago there was the brightest Venus – I think it was Venus – and we got the mini-binoculars out that we have for bird-watching on the reservoirs. There it was this beautiful bright sandy coloured circle. You're not meant to say words like beautiful, that's 'telling not showing'. Find a better word than 'got'. Is it a sonnet yet? (Nothing is shown in a poem, it is all telling. People get confused about distances.) We looked up and then we looked it up. Did you know that Venus is so bright it can cast a shadow on Earth? Or when it rains – sulphuric acid – the droplets can't get to touch the ground because the temperature is so high? The rain evaporates long before that little kiss. But what's that very straight line that goes right across it, like a black sash? We can't find it in any of the pictures. I hand the binoculars to the wee one and he confirms the diagonal. I take up the binoculars again. There it is. A discovery: the new canal of Venus. Certainly not 'natural'. I put the lenses down again. I look up, into the local sky, and see a telephone wire strung across the street and across the rest of the universe.

SHOULDERS

Early hours. His birthday yesterday. Between dreams
he finds his way here, into the bed.
Composite scent: Victoria sponge, vegan sausage rolls.
Something too sweet, an old toffee, a new plastic. He settles,
sleeps splayed, angular. A clothes-horse that's fallen
in the long march back from Moscow.

I can dream, too.
I'm lifting the lad in daylight, lifting him up onto my shoulders.

Half his life ago, we'd stride out like that, gulp up the profligate street.
What is the true meaning of the electronic poster, in mock-glitch?
What is the true meaning of the library's broken light?

I had a knack my friends couldn't repeat: I'd lift this earnest boy
cleanly up, back, over, and there he'd be, shoulder-sentinel, look-out, guard.
It was my only talent. One strong movement. Supple muscles; untrained.

Then we'd move quickly, absurd totem pole, four arms, two heads,
   covering the distance.
We were guardians of ourselves, a carved tree made alive.

> Magpies on the bus shelter, don't worry there's two.
> What's a redwing doing pecking at the leaf litter and latex gloves?
> Why does a gull probe the safety-surface of the open-air gym?
> Why is it solitary?
> Who is playing Howling Wolf? – "Spoonful".
> Is it coming from behind the newspapered window?
> Is it 1976, is it 2010, is it 2050?

Come in, wee one, it was just a nightmare,
or one body remembering another, its warmth.
In the morning I'll tell him: My turn to sit on your shoulders!
He'll look aghast and we'll end up side-by-side, of course, full of questions.

TOTAL CONCENTRATION

when he is almost on his own
playing on the rocks
and he's singing-humming
(I'm not sure how you'd classify it)
total concentration
and his body is moving too
(fluently)   he's dancing

when it's him and me
we're watching an anime
and we both feel the shockwave
the parents have been turned into pigs
serves them right   but even so
and the last train moves through shallow water
incremental inundation   the end of the world by seepage
"I'd love to be on that train, Dad"
"Me too"   "Can we?"

when it's all the family
what's left of it
a wedding   or a Sunday front room
and there he is dancing again
everyone knows he has that gift
celebrate him celebrate us   all life
because everyone had something of that   that gift once
no still does

or so what   keep dancing

THIS WALKING

Back home Hallowe'en is called 'guising',
                  a walking from home to home.
In windows there are eye-and-smile flickers –
                  they're carved into turnips the size of heads.

In this poem of a painting (of a film of a dream of a memory),
you can see how many colours the word 'orange' contains –
lamppost lights, striped roadwork cones,
       a fluorescent tabard over a child's tiger costume, safety armbands,
a carriage-style lamp at a diamond-window front door,
warm light, soft orange curtains. Tangerines, oranges themselves.

In the turnip skulls there are pale candles from the three-day week,
which is "the right thing to do",
                  or "the wrong thing",
or "the wrong way of going about it",
"Do you think freedoms are won without conflict?"

In this poem of a painting
                  (of a film of a dream of a memory),
I'm on the dark doorstep.
I flex my fingers in my father's leather driving gloves, I
stretch the permission of his cream fishing socks over my black school brogues.
Now I
stride out – onto the new tar pavement, onto
                  its scatter of crystal-stone stars,
                    its particular liquorice allsorts.
I wear holes in the fishing-sock wool. (This walking from home to home.)

My best-friend-forever is a troll, so I am a troll.
I have calico ears trimmed with black fur.

My mother has sewed them to a blue-black balaclava
                              I suffer solely on school days.
I wear it only in her field of vision.
Hallowe'en is a decision to open strict doors.

Padding up Churchill Avenue we're entirely on our own
                              ("We are old enough, Mum.").
We have caramel mouths.
We have mocked and forgiven conscientious patrons –
                    for their apples, for the cruelty of a grapefruit.
Now we're about to cross over
              from our neighbourhood of newbuild:
we stop just,
        just,
                /there's a sensation of dense lethal hurriedness/,
just in time –
it's the last lorry in Scotland to carry sacks of coal.

It rushes past us and that second, that second of safety, is a moment forgotten:
on the other side, there's the slink of the first Capri in Scotland.
Each force swaggers past in opposite directions,
                    each weighed down, now, with an old future,
each equalised by lamppost light, an orange-yellow-grey.

In this streetlit poem – of a painting – of a film – of a dream – of a recollection
we decide No
              to the old mansions on the Lochwinnoch Road, turn back
to our own colonized field.
                    "See!" I'll tell my mother,
"We didn't get ourselves killed!"

In this poem of a painting of a film (of a dream, of a memory),
there are different kinds of blue.

Only now, after half a century, do I seem finally

                               to have working ears:

I can hear my mother's precise tenderness

                        in the snip of her embroidery scissors.

Where is my troll? – David Armstrong –

                  you called me Titch, though we could have been twins.

(This walking from home to home.)

You disappeared a week before Christmas.

(He'd said Green could not be my favourite colour

                         and I'd swallowed and said

OK, Blue.)

"His father belongs to the Army, son," my father is telling me, gently.

                               "Re-stationed. It's what

soldiers do."

                                   This walking.

TYRE LEVERS

going back and blue feather green feather pink pink feather a
line of lures feel the weight of each lure son watch the sharp
end the barb a mackerel on each one maybe – fingers – fingers
crossed we've had five on one cast before ask Dave ask Tim
ask your wee brother Rob not too strong on the fishing are
you fold them in now for the journey you've got your own
strengths like tyre levers fold them in into the roll of cloth
where are the tyre levers right now remind me remind me to
check before we head out – just say "Dad, tyre levers" – so I
haven't thought I've packed tyre levers but it's for the fishing
and I definitely have packed tyre levers for the tyres

Before he could write I'd place one of his hands gently on to the blank 'title-page verso' of the birthday card and trace around his fingers. I'd lift his hand off and then write his name on the fingers of the outline, one letter per finger, each letter right at the top where the fingernail would be. He only has four letters in his name so for the thumb I'd write an exclamation mark. Using all the digits seemed pleasing, avoiding a blank cartouche. I'd often do this with him, in notebooks and scraps of paper we had to hand. Soon he'd say his name before I had finished. He seemed to know the vocal tone set by the exclamation mark. "Mum is gonna love this," I'd say and I'd write my message and I'd close the card, wondering if it was too soon, would the ink smudge. I'd bend the card slightly to fit it into the envelope and then seal it all up with two long licks.

Twenty years earlier I had written cards in the same way with my oldest daughter. Her name is five letters long so there was no exclamation mark. By the time she was two we strongly suspected language was going to be very difficult for her. By the time she was three it was a certainty. A blood-test confirmed she had a 'chromosomal deficiency'. It meant even saying a word, never mind writing one, would be impossible. I drew around her fingers and added the letters. She recognised her name spoken out loud so I would say her name as I finished and we'd laugh. Over the years she ceased to co-operate, I think it tickled: she'd withdraw her hand. Another reason is sometimes she prefers to hold.

After her sister was born I'd place little sister's hand within the outline of big sister's. I liked the connection to each other this seemed to give. I see now it was also an expression of the untouching elements of their lives. Soon my younger daughter would be able to write her own name.

I see this text as a card, inserted somewhere into this gathering. If I had the production values I'd reproduce the outline of my own fingers here, write the four-word name my family call me and add an exclamation mark at the thumb. It would be a real card, made of thicker paper and it would have a different colour.

On second thoughts, no, I think it would be better not 'real', not illustrated, not inserted at random. Instead there should be a whole other set of cards interleaved here. They'd fill in the gaps in the narrative, critique each poem, one by one, in hardwearing lamination. Another set (unlimited edition) would be written by all those glimpsed here and there'd be blank ones for readers to fill in: they could keep them for shopping lists if they didn't want to write anything. Finally, there would be a select sample of the cards I've received myself, reproduced in facsimile: Happy Birthday, Happy Father's Day, With Sympathy. Each has been kept for a boost or a hard thought or simply to remember a person through their handwriting.

THREE BOYS AT THE SEA EDGE

As the sea rediscovers a rock pool abandoned only hours ago
I walk with Rory my son towards the far end of the beach.

When he breaks into a sprint I call after him "Rob!"
my little brother and it's forty years ago.

We are racing toward the rock pools.
This time I'll find a way to lose.

WHAT THEY FOUND ON THE BEACH

WHAT THEY FOUND ON THE BEACH

What they found on the beach was a pattern of wreckage,
$\qquad$ wreckage without hierarchy.
There were off-white dice fashioned from light-as-wood bone.
Soldiers in the occupying army rolled them two millennia ago,
resting in the lull they controlled,
throwing them across a surface they had cleared of dust,
$\qquad$ and wishing for personalised luck.

What they found on the beach were red-and-white plastic dice,
fly agaric cute.
They were fashioned in the chancy magic of resuscitated curses, in the era
of oil illness,
$\qquad$ in the age of ecstatic hydrocarbons aflame
$\qquad$ (in the century of self-death).
Soldiers in the occupying army rolled them two days ago,
resting in the lull they thought they controlled, "Nothing personal,"
throwing the dice across a surface cleared of grit –
$\qquad$ wishing for personalised luck.

What I've found again and again on the beach
$\qquad$ is the wedding ring my father once wore.
I'm in a place where only my parents, yet to have children, are present.
Before heading into the water my father leaves – places – the ring
$\qquad$ on the dhobi mark of a laid-out towel.
The stripy cloth's colours, subdued orange and green,
are the colours of tropical fish,
the same creatures who reveal themselves as they're disturbed –
they turn to show their bodies-as-flags
$\qquad$ as my father walks from his shallows to their depths.
Glimpsing their glimmer he thinks *these are real*,
then they are gone, the memory as permanent as a doubt.

Later, as my parents muffle the clink of picnic things into a haversack for
   the road home
the perfect circle of that wedding ring
                    is swept off by my father with a forgetful flick
                    somewhere,
                              anywhere, onto the yellowish beach.
It isn't common for a married man to wear a wedding ring
                      but my father is proud to wear one,
"I'm the luckiest man alive and I don't mind the world knowing it."
Now, in the instant of that single casual movement,
domestic physics – domestic enchantment – has vanished the gold.

A forensic-style search does not recover it.

Finally my mother tugs him away, (up off your hands and knees!),
accepting his ratio of carelessness to devotion.
It is a quiet walk back to the car.
"We'll both laugh about this later," says neither,
though each does smile in the retelling, in time.

What they found high up on the beach, in the rough clutter of the "berm",
                        were chunks of rage, violence solidified.
This is the zone where the drip-drip bickering between ocean and humanity
finally turns ugly, the ugliness of intimacy made grave.
It's a domestic dispute where the weight of past tenderness is used against
   itself,
a drunk but efficient wrestling manoeuvre:
once delicate, shared whispers are now amplified, made jagged –
yells are larger than a thrown fridge.
The sea is flinging the furniture out of its own front window:
ship's engines, Maersk containers the size of chapels, a dredging barge,
                            all are being hurled.
They're landing just short of the trembling road.

What they found high up on the beach was the carcass of a specially
    adapted van,
still with its trailer, all-told the size of a home removals lorry.
It is disguised with a cheerful inscription, still readable: Kaiser's Kaffe.
They were used in the experimental years of a war
to pioneer the gassing of the disabled – adults and children
(those with 'mental illness', the blind, amputees,
those with 'pre-conditions', Down's syndrome).
All with the approval of many in the medical profession, of many in the
    Church,
of many 'right-minded people' even; sometimes, mothers and fathers.

This modest-looking van, with its amateur-looking adaptations,
as if invented by a talented child (using make-do-and-mend household
    appliances),
would be the perfect test-case for 'categories of humans' – how to make
    them vanish –

thousands, millions,
as many perhaps as the sum of golden sand grains in a well-built sandcastle,

and now what I find on the beach, which is calm now, for the moment,
                            is my late mother and father,
                                        fully alive,
        helping their sons and their families build just such castles,
and I'm helping my daughters and son to build just such a castle,
a fairy-tale citadel – perfectly-shaped,
                        with high walls, a flag and four turrets.
"Shall we have a moat?" my son says, and I say
                        "Yes, and let's build a canal to the waves."
He tells me: "We could own half the sea!"
We cut the trench and wait for the surge.

SHORE GIFTS

GULLS

At the sea-edge, the junk team,
the cleanliness collective.

Immaculate.

The curse for being owed admiration
is thanklessness.

LIMPET

A firm grasp of its future: life as mouth.

HERMIT CRAB

Wherever I lay my hat, that's my home.

MOON JELLYFISH

The knowledge of no controlling intelligence. Unsettling, unsettled.

Botched blooms in the berm's clefts. Snipped tie-dyes, soft-purple, in clear
mush.

Neon elements out of their element, stranded gelatin, fly-tipped implants,
purple rind.

LEAP YEAR JELLYFISH

light after light after light after light after light after light after light after
light after light after light after light after light after light after light after
light after light after light after light after light
light after light after light after light after light after light after light after
light after light after light

SUNGLASSES

Land-crab for faces.

SUNCREAM

This treaty is formally ratified with a solemn ceremony: you splat my back, I splat yours.

ICE CREAM CONE

Olympic torch, champion of dawdle. Got this one licked.

FISH AND CHIPS

Unfold the lagoony map and no need for clues.
The chips are ingots. Cod, priceless, is pursed in wrinkling gold.

SUMMER READING

Souvenir recipes by a grilled face. The graphic novel of Finnegans Wake, murder in the AirBnB: now rate your host.

Chicklit and the solace of a new history of in-between spaces. Inspector Rebus with the last ten pages razored out.

Grease spots and honey and corners of pages turned down, a receipt for kids go free. The complete undiscovered on Kindle. Was Shakespeare Shakespeare?

SEA ANEMONE, CLOSED

In the rock-pool, a deep red nub. Shy, swollen.

SAND DAM

Ambition is engineering. There will be a wall
to hold your childhood in: backed up to footprints, overwhelmed.

Transparent shrimp / serene foetus.

Freshwater. The immense scale
of first memories and now a new remember,
                                    lovers on each side
patting the levee, last sand in place.

The dam bursts and everyone is more than alive.

PEDALO DREAMS

Pocket paddle-steamer. Pedestrians as pilot and puff.
"Pedal harder, we're partners!"

I can see Penzance.

                                                    "I can see Peru."

LOSING THE WORD 'LOVE'

LOSING THE WORD 'LOVE'

I
need so
much better
for you Mum. No,
I will say "Mother"

to respect the laughter
and Star Trek transfers which glow
green/yellow long seconds after
the light switch clicks and the dark you know

is held by gifts for this small child off school –
a broken eardrum, was it, or 'daymare flu'?
I can't say love – that word's too many kinds of true –
catch-all for like, for lust, breaker of its own proud rule:

that love's select. Love's too full. I'll love you until I die.

CHOKE RISK

I
have not
finished yet.
The air is hot,
thick with kapok, debt,

this choke risk. I exist
because of you, what you'd lend
of yourself, or give, that long list.
I still receive your gifts, want to send

these letters in thanks and awe. They're just here,
and I have more – I could 'slip them beneath the door'
but don't. I won't attempt to force them to appear
on your side. They're distorted prayers and god knows what for.

I hope you knew how loved you were before they let you die.

I CAN'T SEE EITHER

I
can't see
either why
now so late I
have to disagree

with myself. After all
this time – your life long past –
loss still pulses up. Sleepless call
to what? Your memory could not last:

holding fast, attempting still to know you,
(most details lost), and ending knowing the blanks
stay blank for 'good' – that is more than this son can do,
a dark task. A wicked stepmother wouldn't ask. Thanks,

thanks, replace grief, abstract gratitude but deep; backward high.

SPOOLY, DREEP

Standing right on top of the wall with two new words to keep.
Standing high on it all and thinking cock of the heap.
Standing like a graph with all my brothers in line.
Sharing the laugh and the symbol and the sign.
Standing like I said tootin the full toot.
Victory on the edge with all that fruit.

(My mother's miles away, as Mum.
Damsons are the truest plum –
as sharp as sharp does seep,
rare, they say, as sleep.)

Four boys crouch low,
hang hard, deep.
Push,
            throw,

                     leap.

GIRL OF SLENDER MEANS

My mother could always escape –
lithe, and just short of tall.

Her boyfriend had been killed
in a children's war

a children's war
out in the burning East.

Wounded, contorted,
she still shimmied, slipped out

strong enough to find her second choice.
She'd love him,

in rooms she checked for second exits,
until she woke, helpless

(a late diagnosis),
husband and sons

looming in the door frame,
windows jammed shut

with trivial paint,
and a fever that burned the house to the ground.

4711: ECHT KÖLNISCH WASSER

In the gallery of faces there's only one face.

You can ask too much of a mother, living not to live,
adept at J-cloth death.

There's a song stainless steel amplifies –
a three-word chorus microphoned by mixer tap.

Is it I love you? Is it Sink sink sink?

> (A perfume my mother was alive with.
> "With which my mother.")

ZERO HOURS, THE VAST HORSE
for Ellie

she
can't see
family –
the boss calls or
does not call and she
texts Soz, can't. Miss u guys

the
sultan
of delete
owns owns owns and
pays or doesn't pay
sorry system error
week to ten days no longer

                    the
                    control
                    she commands

                    the vast horse   snatched reins
                    the jumps   the trials

Please petrol
money please please
luv u dad serious

I WOULD LIKE TO MEET PEOPLE

I would like to meet people I have never met before.

I would like to meet my mother,
        as if she had lived beyond my twenty-third year.
'Twenty something' is still a child of a kind,
        as I have learned from my own children.
Now that her sons were all leaving home
        she had just taken up painting again
so perhaps we could visit exhibitions together
                        and both find new influences,
and she could tell me where she trained
and what the ideas about art were in those days,
and what was the argument her father had with the Army?

I'd tell my mother just enough about poetry not to put her off
and most of all we'd just laugh, and in the galleries she'd make that half-
    cough of hers
when she ventured into something risqué, or simply sensual.

I would like to meet my eldest child
as if she hadn't been born with catastrophic chromosomes.
We all need at least to try to accept our own shapes and dance patterns
        and the shapes and patterns of those around us:
yes, yes, we should all celebrate what there is to be celebrated – there is so
    much, even so –
but I do notice her exact contemporaries
        and admire their articulacy with a phone,
their breaking and making of friendships, their conspiracies,
and I know my daughter, who will always be approximately 1 in 'mental years',
would have loved to be among them.
Like them, she'd keep that certain distance from her father,
        who doesn't know anything about the real world.

I would like to meet the woman I called the love of my life,
a phrase which stands in severe reproach to me.
I used it in earnest when we were lovers
        but I failed the gravity of its declaration, merely heart-felt.
I am ashamed.
I would like to meet her as if the stroke which paralyses her to this day
        had not gripped her, suddenly, inexplicably,
                a week before our seventh Feast of St Valentine.
In the years after, her illness tested me and I did not pass that test.

These days, sometimes, we help each other to visit exhibitions.
We navigate the frustrations of the 'modern transport network'.
These are well-known to anyone dependant on the use of a wheelchair
                but apparently hidden to everyone else.
We are still surprised together – did you know Duchamp was a sensitive
  portrait-maker,
or how soothing the 'target' paintings of Jasper Johns can be?

I think of the mother I knew only for a short while, how she would have
  liked these gallery visits, too,
and, since there is visual skill in the family, I wonder if my daughter,
if she had not been 'blessed' with distorted DNA, might have been an
  artist as well –
              she might well have liked to come along.
She would have wanted to know
        what was the argument her great grandfather had with the Army?

Too, too, too. The longing in loss's could-have-beens, the yearning in shadow
  additions.

I would like to meet the people close to me who I have never met before,
though somehow while still being close to all the actual people I am lucky
  to know
who have been part-created by random acts of natural violence

and by how, generally speaking, the world has treated them since;
by how, specifically speaking, I have treated them since.

Perhaps we would all travel more, separately, together, I don't know in
   what combinations
(managing two wheelchairs at one time is a task and a half,
      but we'd be helped comprehensively in this well-staffed daydream).
Beyond this almost useless geography
                    of longing and guilt and regret,
we'd meet 'real' people as if we were all real, too.

In the gentle tourism I imagine, not one of those we encountered
               would be a person we had met before,
and I bet almost everyone would like to hear my mother's explanation:
what was the argument her father had with the Army?

SHORE THEFTS

'HAUL YOUR PAPER SHIPS UP'
after Montale

Haul your paper ships up the scorched shore
and then sleep, little-boy captain –

may you never hear the evil spirits
sailing now in flocks.

(In the walled garden
the owl's had enough.
The smoke from the rooves
lies heavy.

The work of months is a ruin.
The moment arrives
and it cracks in secret, bursts with a puff.)

The collapse is coming.
Maybe without a sound.
The architects can sense
their death sentence.
Time to save
their little jug of cream,
it even looks like a miniature boat,
just that.

Tie your fleet up
in the hedges.

BODIES

the light warm bodies at the top of the sandy beach
are sympathetic to   are shocked by   object to
the cold dense the cold dense dark bodies   at the tideline

the light warm bodies at the top of the sandy beach
are sympathetic by   are shocked of   object in

the warm bodies
the cold bodies

the light warm bodies at the top of the beach
are sympathetic to   are shocked by   object to
"think about it" the cold dark bodies

"they couldn't have been refugees they had phones."

the dead are coming here to take our jobs

GAZA
Zakariya, Ismail, Mohammad, and Ahed Rest in Peace

Just playing hide and seek among the beach huts, then a bit of
footie on the sand.

"All delete games insert conflicts (can we say conflicts?) all
disputes have rules, measurement, proportionality. Oldest
11, youngest 9. Measurement important. Totally exonerated,
anyone would have, -- couldn't quite see the kill / console,
that's my story and I'm, why take risk of four insert threatening
delete unarmed delete four children insert men delete playing.
Delete four children."

DOG WHELK ON A LIMPET

The helix is elegance and strength. We are blessed.

The process is simple and cannot hurt the animal.
An individual climbs onto the grazing beast and secures a position.
With our power limb we rasp at a single point in its armour,
                              scraping the calcium down to a filament.
Once the drilling has all but compromised the shell our mouth takes over:
we apply hydrochloric saliva to the weak spot
      and soon our seeking lips push through the last layer into the flesh
      and organs.
The mouth we are graced with is a variety of limb itself, a probe if you like,
and so we reach in, in, kissing every organ of the animal –
I believe they accept and even enjoy this –
applying enzymes and acid as we do, liquefying every quarter of the creature.

It is one of life's great pleasures.

Finally, our ever-versatile mouth becomes a drinking straw.
The slurry makes the most refreshing of soups.

TAMPON

Toxic shock on the ebb-tide.
Stringed chum in shark week.

WET WIPES

Strong as a choking sensation.
Long-lasting moist and no fuss.
Babies get rectangles.

CONDOM

Ecstatic membrane, as was. Creature of the deep.
As like to joy as regret, as like to love as squalor.

(Stretch of delirium, doom of the micro-fish.)

GHOST GEAR

Truth is it's fishermen and writers in mobile factories, in supply-chain
    mouths,
killing the sea: the deaths are from lines and lines, the illusion
    of wholesome,
chains of hydrocarbon ink, evasions. Correction: super-rich cries
    of ways of life.

TOTAL IMMERSION

There, present from spume to sea-floor, the debris of a fact: the weight of
the plastic exceeds the weight of the fish.

ABRADED SYNTHETICS

(How fish breathe water and abraded synthetics,
as if our lungs could take gulp after gulp of sump oil
and the dust from 'protect-my-child' school-run tyres).

LAGOS

Regal Sea View beach: Kids Clean Club, Beach Samaritans.

MICROBEADS

Infinite abacus
broken, stuffed into Earth's gut.

Survival:
        don't count on it.

INVISIBLES

Painkillers / oestrogen at scale in the thickening water. Slicks of
neat fertility from industrialised farms. Desolation correctors
beyond correction. Numbness and 'economic growth'.

CASTS

When they first saw the wobbly spirals in the grey sand they said this is a script for a new language. We discovered it and we will teach ourselves to speak it. (Talk and fond glances as light as sea-spray).

Later, trying to rescue themselves, they learned casts are waste products. The worms have made their homes just beneath the surface of well it's not sand it's mud.

VOYEUR

It's not lust it's boredom. People-watching, the unregulated end.
Failure to organise the rounded life: bad luck, he tells himself, way back.

Availability of chances for petty glimpses.
The second cove, they're hand in hand,
then glans and Glenda.

He won't look, he does look.

Near lethargy of sly and now it's 'spiritual.'

SLUICE FRUIT

A wild swim: the quality of arse-gravy cannot be strained. Large croutons, small dung dumplings; anus apples turning in the swell; blood-streaked polio potatoes in dripping; toilet tofu; brown-yellow crusts in the dark swill; freemarket floaters in the filth of foam.

POOL OVERLOOKING THE BAY

Paradise is an oblong of lo-chlor, waveless.
Idealise a cove with aqua and non-slip.

Thanks to waterproof streaming the rockless rockpool has dance:
CHOOON!

WILDFIRES REACH THE SEA-VIEW MANSIONS

Heli-pad, but the pilot is stuck in traffic. Live by the drill, die by the
drought.

EVEN SO, THIS CLOSENESS

Saunter together in the shallows, just they two, waves above their thighs.
The good silence, tensionless. Relaxed generosity of let it be. Look, said in
the low voice of the naturalist, look. A huge speckled flatfish, is it a plaice
is it a flounder is it a ray, it's not a shadow.

MESSAGE IN A PLASTIC BOTTLE

How would you like your world? Sparkling or still?

AFTER WORDS

ARE YOU STILL THERE?

Are you still there? –
The sea is talking in its sleep,
fond names, and no blame each.
The sea would crush you, but you keep it in reach.

Are you still there? –
The sea is singing in its sleep,
hard tunes, songs ground from speech.
The sea would crush you, but you think it's here to teach.

Not every question sees the light on the hill.
Not every question gleans the spoil from the spill.
Do you think a question will keep the waves still?
(If yours won't, no one else's will.)

Are you still there? –
The sea is turning in its sleep,
stone dreams and bodies on the beach.
The sea would crush you, but you keep it in reach.

Are you still there?

IN OUR NATURE

Yes
to trees
and a dream –
of a future.

Shared dreams, like ghosts, are
in our nature.
                    We see
dark trees, sometimes, trapped in sleep.
We plant bright trees, we rebuild a

failed city. It's then we glimpse the ghosts
the last forests still keep. Who they are and

what they tell is beyond all pity: they're souls
from razed woods and our children's children after death.

WEDDING SONG

It's all in the eyes –
the glimpses, yes,
the astonishment of presence
and then full open eyes, the long look
(the laughing look, the connecting look)
eyes that know and share and love

It's all in the hands,
the miracle of hand-in-hand, yes
hands seeking hands,
a caring hand on a shoulder,
working hands at rest, side by side,
hands that know and share and love

It's all in the understanding
'getting to know' takes a lifetime, yes,
life of the closest understandings
the elaborate luck
the gift of finding
and all to know and share and love

THEY LIVE WITHOUT US

They live without us,
unconcerned.

Roadsides know them,
don't know.

Call or song or
pattern of presence.

Our senses worn down,
could be alive,

working on it.

A mark
and then nothing.

DINOSAUR

This is a small wooden dinosaur.
It's a brontosaurus, "Thunder Lizard", one of the vast creatures in the
    diplodocus family,
all herbivores (I've read about this).

It's a 'gentle giant' in my uncle's lyrical render, silent.
The silence is important, though you might say all sculpture is silent.
Perhaps, but this is certainly a peaceful work, an elegant work, yes, gentle.
It is keeping me company at this moment and though you could say I am
    distracted by it
by talking about it now, it is not interrupting me. There is no serenity like
    this.
It's keeping the kind of silence I was always told, soflty, to keep
                                        when a companion to my father.
Like my uncle he was a skilled angler. Quiet was a law.
Once, aged six or seven, I stood in the wrong place
and when, to cast, he whipped his line back, he hooked me in the cheek,
    just beneath my eye.
Even then I tried silence but I did cry out.

I believe my Uncle Rob was an engineer on the railways.
I have belief in unsolved memories.
On one occasion he taught me to calculate the speed of any train.
You'd use your wristwatch to time a count of certain way-markers at the
    side of the tracks.
In the same way that I've forgotten the calculation that revealed the
    velocity of the train,
so the industry has erased the way-markers themselves,
but I can remember that sensation, when the average speed was known,
of becoming a physical entity again, connected properly to the reality
of the canals and the enchanted specific buildings which trains as they
    pass offer

and then withhold.

(Sheets of shaped grey metal as architecture, and stark uses beyond casual
  comprehension.)

Today speed is divined digitally, for the purposes of driver and marketing
only,

opaque to even skilled observers.

I imagine a future in which there is the planting of trees at regular
  intervals trackside –

all are taught from childhood how to measure the speed of superfast trains
                                        by the timing of trees.

I know just planting trees is a child-like response to the emergency,

and there are always problems

with leaves on the line, but if it all gets through planning

in this way citizen passengers will help to re-green the world

and they can re-exist as bodies in real space with their uncles

who don't need now to teach their nephews or nieces these calculations, it
  will just be known.

Instead, children can settle down to play poker dice – the other gift my
  uncle gave me

(in a narrow see-through wallet, so the dice's royal faces
  were like passengers in windows).

All can while away a journey across countries
                                  with the heavier-than-sugar-cube visages –

knaves, kings, queens, all their heads thrown across a formica table.

My uncle carved the dinosaurs in different sizes.

The largest our family had, still only the size of a kitten,

used to stand on the sill of the long window of our front room.

It was guarding against any sheep tempted to exploit Scotland's no-tres-
  pass laws.

This would occur whenever the river was in spate.

Suddenly their pasture would be reduced to mossy lawns and lavender.

Of course, the brontosaurus was a vegetarian, but the sheep didn't use the library.

When my mother died Uncle Rob had been dead for several years. I

am trying to say this poetically but I am trying to say this truthfully.
Each I think of my brothers was given one of his dinosaurs –
we seemed to have just enough to go round.
I'm tentative about this since all was confusion and in one home I've not
    seen a sculpture.
I don't want to ask. It could be a sensitive point. Please don't pass word
    on.
For the most part, when we see them in each other's homes I think we
    know we are connected,
(we know this already, but when we see them we *know* this, it is at the
    front of the mind),
and we remember our closeness and the distance of our uncle
all that way from a suburb of Glasgow to a suburb in the Welsh borders.
To visit, my elder brothers would accompany my father in a fast car –
    a brand new Capri.
They'd be dropped off for a long weekend of carp and canoes
but my younger brother and I stayed close,
we were sculpted more by our mother (and public transport).

Today we are now distant uncles to our nephews and nieces, some at least. I

am trying to explain this – get the facts right –
I'm trying to stylise this – get the lines right. I'm trying –
We are physically distant brothers now,
all that way from a suburb of Glasgow to a suburb of Sydney.
We travel digitally, through facetime, and we are mostly prosaic, like this
    poem.
We talk with each other about groceries and graves
                        (and see a dinosaur in the background, or its absence).
We laugh and glitch.

(For a time, palaeontologists had second thoughts about the brontosaurus
– its first discovery was discovered to be a misclassification, just an
    amalgam of foreign bones.
(I am an amalgam of foreign bones).
But decades later, 'Big Data helped Big Grazer':
a presence was discovered there, distinct.)

My small sculpture is in dark wood, mahogany perhaps.
    It's a memento mori now.
Yes, so much time has passed and I haven't managed to see
                            the way-markers, to understand the speed, to feel it,

but this little object has become a way-marker itself.
It's as if a single instance, a small elegantly-shaped copy
of a spirit of a force many millions of years deceased,
could, alone, gather knowledge of the small humans around it,
and itself be slight enough to slip through physics, allow a measure to be
    taken,
allow us to be re-bodied in memory and in future ideals.

I have moved home, perhaps for the last time, just the boy and me,
and here is a dinosaur, unpacked again.

LAST WORD

PERSONALITY TEST
with worked examples

Are you made of dogs, fogs, or cogs?
Son: dogs.
Father: fogs.

Are you made of cats, splats, or rats?
Son: splats.
Father: cats/rats.

Are you made of sticks, tricks, or licks?
Father: tricks.
Son: licks.

Are you lights, tights, or fights?
Father: lights.
Son: fights
Son: you're tights.
Father: lights.
Son: he's tights.

Are you bones, phones, or moans?
Father: phones.
Son: moans

Are you playing, saying, or neighing?
Son: saying.
Father: neighing

Are you made of coasts, boasts, or ghosts?
Son: coasts.
[   ]
Father: ghosts

Are you made of board games, band names, or old flames?
Father: band names / old flames.
Son: board games

Are you a note pad, an iPad, or a launch pad?
Father: a launch pad.
Son: iPad.
Son: he's a note pad.

Are you country walks, serious talks, magic bean stalks?
Son: serious talks.
Father: You are not serious talks! You are magic bean stalks.
Son: serious talks.
[   ]
Father: I'm country walks.

Do you practise stagecraft, witchcraft, or Minecraft?
Father: witchcraft.
Son: Minecraft

Are you asks, tasks, or masks?
Son: asks.
Father: tasks/masks.

Are you sneezes, teases, or pleases?
Father: teases / pleases
Son: sneezes.

Are you afraid of locks, rocks, or socks?
Son: locks.
Father: locks
Father: you're also afraid of socks.
Son: just locks.